D1518751

Polar Bears

Leo Statts

abdopublishing.com

Published by Abdo Zoom™, PO Box 398166, Minneapolis, Minnesota 55439. Copyright © 2017 by Abdo Consulting Group, Inc. International copyrights reserved in all countries. No part of this book may be reproduced in any form without written permission from the publisher. Abdo Zoom™ is a trademark and logo of Abdo Consulting Group, Inc.

Printed in the United States of America, North Mankato, Minnesota
062016
092016

Cover Photo: Kotomiti Okuma/Shutterstock Images, cover
Interior Photos: Iakov Filimonov/Shutterstock Images, 1; iStockphoto, 4, 8, 12–13; Frank Hildebrand/iStockphoto, 5; Andre Anita/iStockphoto, 6, 16; Derek Dammann/iStockphoto, 7; Kenneth Canning/iStockphoto, 9; Josef Friedhuber/iStockphoto, 10–11; Mike Schumann/iStockphoto, 11; Red Line Editorial, 13, 20 (left), 20 (right), 21 (left), 21 (right); Sarkophoto/iStockphoto, 14; Cindy Haggerty/iStockphoto, 15; Keith Szafranski/iStockphoto, 17; John Pitcher/iStockphoto, 18, 19

Editor: Emily Temple
Series Designer: Madeline Berger
Art Direction: Dorothy Toth

Publisher's Cataloging-in-Publication Data
Names: Statts, Leo, author.
Title: Polar bears / by Leo Statts.
Description: Minneapolis, MN : Abdo Zoom, [2017] | Series: Polar animals |
    Includes bibliographical references and index.
Identifiers: LCCN 2016941135 | ISBN 9781680791891 (lib. bdg.) |
    ISBN 9781680793574 (ebook) | ISBN 9781680794465 (Read-to-me ebook)
Subjects: LCSH: Polar bear--Juvenile literature.
Classification: DDC 599.786--dc23
LC record available at http://lccn.loc.gov/2016941135

Table of Contents

Polar Bears

Polar bears live in the Arctic.
Their fur is thick and white.

It keeps them warm in icy waters.

Body

Polar bears have large bodies.

They have big paws. Their claws are sharp.

Polar bears have black skin.
It soaks up heat from the sun.

Under their skin is a
layer of fat. It traps heat.
This keeps the bear warm.

Polar bears live near frozen **coasts**.
They walk on sea ice.
They swim in chilly water.

Polar bears dig **dens**.
The dens protect them
from cold weather.

Where polar bears live

Food

Polar bears are **predators**.
They eat meat.
They mostly eat seals.

Sometimes seals are hard
to find. So polar bears will eat
almost any food.

Polar bears have babies in a den. The babies are called **cubs**.

16

Polar bears often have **twins**.

Cubs leave their mothers
after two years.

Polar bears can live up to 30 years in the wild.

19

Average Length

A polar bear is longer than a sofa.

7 ft 6 in

7 ft

Average Weight

A polar bear weighs more than a soda vending machine.

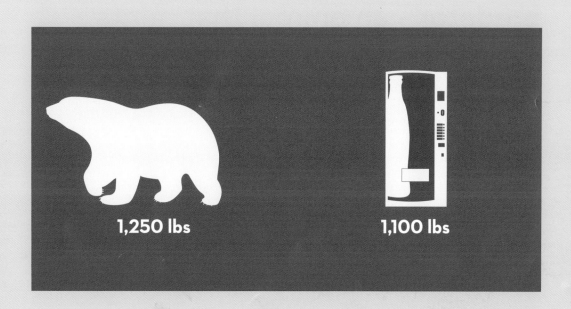

1,250 lbs   1,100 lbs

Glossary

coast - land near a body of water.

cub - a young animal.

den - a hidden place for animals to live or hibernate.

predator - an animal that hunts others.

twins - two animals born together from one mother.

Booklinks

For more information
on **polar bears**, please visit
booklinks.abdopublishing.com

Zoom In on Animals!

Learn even more with the Abdo Zoom
Animals database. Check out
abdozoom.com for more information.

Index

24